As you Read this Book. May the [...]
& Revelation of Go[...] [...]ly
& Business!
Ki[...]

ACR; [...]

AWAKENING
THE KINGDOM
WITHIN YOU

Corey T. Ricks &
Tisha Ricks, CPC.

ACKNOWLEDGMENT

We want to thank Our King of Kings and Lord of Lords, The Holy Spirit; our governor, teacher, helper, & truth giver for bringing us out of the shadows of religion and awakening us to what it means to operate in the Kingdom and how to manifest it "in earth as it is in heaven."

We want to thank our anointed children, Trevon & Courtney Ricks, for being partners with us on this amazing journey. We know it hasn't been easy, but it's been well worth it!

TABLE OF CONTENTS

PREFACE

Why do many in the Church experience few victories in life? The simple answer is because they don't realize that God has put the power to succeed and make a major impact on the world around them inside them. As the saying goes, "until one goes *within*, they will always do without."

It's not our devotion alone that causes the best of God's Kingdom to be added to our life; knowing the purpose we're created for and putting it into action is the key to success and victory. "Faith without works is dead", says James 2:17.

Our hearts became burdened by the condition of those who did not succeed but professed Jesus as their Lord and Savior and served in His Church, yet there was a disconnect! Where was the tangible manifestation of His power in their lives? Why were so many not prospering and always claiming they were waiting on God to do something? According to the word of God, He gave us the power and the ability to do (Ephesians 3:20). Even in our own lives, we seemed to be the "tail in many situations and not the head, usually beneath and not above" (Deuteronomy 28:13). There was an unrest and an unfulfillment inside us! We needed to address it so that we could move forward and begin to experience "life more abundantly" as the King promised and the way He intended.

Many were *preaching* faith, and everybody seemed to be talking about faith. However, not many *moved out* in faith like in the stories of the great patriarchs throughout the word of God. The burden on our spirits and souls became intense, and the Holy Spirit spoke that it was our turn to be an example of what it truly means to "walk by faith and not by sight." So, through us, Kingdom Reformation Ministries Worldwide came into existence to teach and demonstrate how to live as a productive citizen "on earth as it is in heaven."

At the most 'inconvenient' moment (or so we thought), He gave us a promise that told us to read Deuteronomy 8, and said if we stayed where we were, we would DIE there. We began to pack all our belongings—which at the time were two bags full of clothes and our two small children—and were told to go to a land that He would show us, and that land was Georgia. We had NO money, but a ride willing to take us and provide what we needed in that moment. The circumstances were NOT ideal, but we took what He had provided at that moment as a sure sign that He had spoken, and all we needed to do was follow. In 1 Kings 17:7, Elijah was told to move on because the brook had dried up. That was our reality at that moment, so we had no option but to move to where He was leading us. After all, the safest and only place to be is in the perfect will and presence of God!

That began our journey to discovering and being **AWAKENED TO THE KINGDOM WITHIN** us. We believe this book will stand as the catalyst you need to provoke you to come out of the shallowness of just being a "good Christian" and into being a bonafide Kingdom citizen whose life is marked by power, dominion, authority, fruitfulness, and demonstration; because you have gained an understanding, and are willing to rise up and do what the King has assigned to you.

INTRODUCTION

There's a point in life when every creature on the face of the planet must come out of an unconscious state of being, and there's a natural state every human must experience in order to function properly. This state is called *sleep*; but what is sleep? According to Webster's dictionary, it is the natural periodic suspension of consciousness during which the powers of the body are restored.

In other words, it's necessary for humans to have regular periods of sleep for the body to be regenerated and to operate at its optimal levels.

However, in this state of suspended consciousness, there are many limitations on our state of being, from the inability to decipher fiction from reality, to the inability to think and reason, to physically being in a constrained position—usually lying down. There is a given moment when one must awaken from sleep, because to stay there would be the end of all things...death.

Many, especially in the body of Christ, have remained in a sleeplike state of unconsciousness even in their waking lives. As a result, everything in and around their lives resembles death, and they can't figure out why, or how to fix it. Until they do, living life the way God intended for them to live it remains a hope and a dream, never their reality. Proverbs 13:12 tells us that "hope deferred makes the heart sick, but a longing fulfilled is a tree of life." Many in the body of Christ have grown sick because they must awaken from the false beliefs that many "Christian" teachings have sold to them. Through it, people have been made to believe the direct opposite of what Christ our King came to Earth to reveal and establish. His message was, as it is given in Matthew 3:2, to "repent, for the **kingdom** of heaven is at hand." To repent means to make a 360-degree turn in another direction; towards the Kingdom and away from the powerless and oppressing rules and rudiments of religion. Until this happens in the life of an individual who names Christ as their Lord and Savior, they will walk through life with their "eyes wide shut" until they awaken to what Christ the King came to earth preaching, teaching, and demonstrating to make them FREE! "If the son therefore make you free, you shall be free indeed!" (John 8:36).

This Is What's Been Missing

Luke 17:20-21, "the kingdom of God does not come with observation, nor will they say, see here or see there; for indeed, the kingdom of God is **within** you". Jesus said that the kingdom of God does not come with observation, so if we cannot witness it with sight, then we must witness it by revelation, and that cannot be obtained without a renewal of the mind.

If the kingdom of God is within us, the power of the Holy Spirit is available to us; and we can tap into it by faith to put this power into action in our lives.

Paul said in 2 Corinthians 5:20 "now then, we are ambassadors for Christ." If we are ambassadors for Christ, then everything that we need will come from the country that we belong to, and God has put His kingdom right inside of us. Our citizenship is not earthly, but heaven-bound, so we cannot use the tools of this world righteously to prosper. Our prosperity comes from heaven, and comes about when God gives us concepts, ideas, and insights. He has given each of us a talent that we will prosper from, but we need to have a renewal of the mind to receive His revelation and wisdom and access it. The Kingdom of God is not limited to monetary prosperity; it consists of every good thing that we need or desire, and tapping into it hinges on a renewed view of the way that God thinks. Philippians 2:5 says it this way: "Let this mind be in you, which was also in Christ Jesus."

If we want to have our minds renewed, we cannot serve both God and mammon; we cannot live our lives partly in this world and partly in the Kingdom of God, because the two do not mix. "Choose ye this day whom you will serve!"

What does it mean to have a renewal of the mind?

It simply means to change the way that we think and begin to think the way that God thinks. We have to conform our way of thinking to His before the Kingdom of God can begin to manifest in our lives.

Jesus not only came to die for our sins, but also to show us the Father; prior to His coming people had only had a glimpse of God, and only a few had had a personal relationship with Him, but Jesus made God visible to everyone who wanted to know Him.

From the moment that we become born again, the Kingdom of God dwells in us, but that does not mean that it takes over our lives. Rather, we have to renew our minds. Ephesians 4:22-23 encourages us to "put off concerning your former conduct, the old man which grows corrupt according to the deceitful lusts and be renewed in the spirit of your mind".

There are many Christians who are sick today; and there are many experiencing various forms of lack in their lives even with the Kingdom of God living inside of them. It makes one wonder what is the problem? Why are so many of God's people suffering? The answer is simple; *their minds are not renewed.*

Yes, they are saved because they have accepted Jesus as their Lord and Savior, but something is missing; they are not experiencing what they can have in Him! The sad thing is, it is already in them to receive.

When the Lord comes into our life, He does not come empty-handed. In fact, the word says that His gifts are before Him, so when Jesus comes into our lives, the Kingdom of God comes with Him, and that is a gift.

In our walk of faith, He will not break any of His promises unto us. "He will not withhold any good thing from us." Jesus said, "whatsoever we desire when we pray to believe that we have received it and we will have it." He did not say to believe that we are *going* to receive it, He said to believe that we *have* received it. Why? Because it is already inside of us!

When we know that the Kingdom of God is inside of us, we will no longer say, "I am believing God for this or that". Instead, we'll say "I have it!" and thank Him for giving it to us before we see it in our physical reality. That is our faith! When we speak that way, the thing that we desire will arise from the Kingdom that is inside of us and will be manifested openly. Also, when we know that the Kingdom of God is inside us, we will know that we are victorious in everything, because there is no defeat in His Kingdom.

Chapter 1

WHAT IS THE KINGDOM?

The Kingdom is not some complex mystery, as some would have you believe. It is simply the *Government of God*, established through the life and lifestyles of those in the body of Christ. We are called to exemplify Jesus Christ's character and nature for He is the head of this government. Isaiah 9:6 gives us a glimpse of this; "For unto us a child is born, unto us a son is given: and the government shall be upon His shoulder: and His name shall be called Wonderful, Counselor, The Mighty God, The Everlasting Father, The Prince of Peace."

In this Kingdom, or Government, we must be willing to follow and obey the leading of our governor and teacher, who is the Holy Ghost. We must trust Him to wholeheartedly govern our lives. By doing so, we will be endowed and equipped with wisdom, power, and the authority to effectively operate within our government's statutes, precepts, and principles, and to carry out our King's agenda. These things are clearly written within the word of God, which is our government's constitution—the fundamental framework of how the government operates and outlines what our King requires.

We are able to communicate with our King by way of prayer, and this allows our Kingdom's legislation to be enforced in the Earth realm. When this happens, the plans and purpose of the kingdom of darkness will be thwarted, and more citizens can begin to be added to the Kingdom of God! More souls can be won for our King, and an increased number of laborers raised up to go out into His harvest field. Matthew 9:38 gives a clear reference to this when it states "therefore pray earnestly to the Lord of the harvest to send out laborers into His harvest."

By now, it should be crystal clear that the Kingdom and Government of God is not outside of us, but is rather within us! Any teaching that does not align with this understanding is contrary to the word of God.

Let us make reference to the aforementioned scripture again to make sure we now have a better understanding of this truth. Luke 17:20-21 says "And when He (Jesus) was demanded of the Pharisees, when the kingdom of God should come, He answered them and said, the kingdom of God cometh not with observation: Neither shall they say, Lo here! or, lo there! for, behold, the kingdom of God is within you."

Jeremiah 1:5 of our kingdom's constitution causes us to awaken to the truth that each individual has a pre-destined purpose. "Before I formed you in the womb I knew you, before you were born I set you apart; I appointed you as a prophet to the nations."

This shows that *every* individual—be they believer or unbeliever—has the Kingdom within them. They just have to become conscious of it. For the believer satisfied with just going to a church and doing religious activities, doing so will not awaken them to this reality...

The Ultimate Reality

The Kingdom of God is the ultimate reality. Psalm 24:1 says that "the earth is the Lord's, and the fullness thereof; the world, and they that dwell therein." Essentially, that which is part of the Earth is part of the Kingdom, for all creation is the Lord's work. However, while the reality of the Kingdom is clear in other dimensions, it is obscured on planet Earth! Because you are a resident of this human plane, it is obscured from you and your work while you are here, so you must pull away from the trappings that hide it to reveal its majesty to your own consciousness.

"The Kingdom of God is within you," reveals the basic truth about the dilemma of human existence, expecially when we take into account the saying that goes "what's out of sight is out of mind." The kingdom is at hand, and is right where you are. You are within it, just as it is within you; and you need only to accept it, but to do so, you must begin to understand it.

You Are Always in the Kingdom

A very simple analogy is to compare the existence of the Kingdom to the life-giving properties of air on the earth plane. You cannot see the air, and yet it must be there, for you cannot live without it.

You live in the midst of it and require it for the maintenance of your being; and yet you seldom think about it or focus on it, even though it is always there and necessary for your existence.

In the same manner, you are always in the Kingdom, and the Kingdom is always in you, even though you are not consciously aware of it. As you come to understand your relationship with the earth and the air, you will also understand the concept of the Kingdom.

Doing so requires detachment from human consciousness to the extent that you can see it and understand it for what it is—even while you continue to live in it—as well as total acceptance of the true reality of your being.

For now, know that you are making good progress on the journey to true understanding. Persevere— no matter the circumstances—and maintain an attitude of hope, trust, and acceptance. Your efforts to make your dreams come true and realize your goals on the Earth's plane are part of your effort to understand the Kingdom and to reside consciously in it, for the Kingdom is perfection, and it is the ultimate reality.

An Heir to the Kingdom

You are an heir to the Kingdom of God, which is total goodness, and you totally deserve it all. Never doubt this for an instant! If you grasp nothing else from this lesson, please do not miss this insight.

Chapter 2

SEEKING THE KINGDOM OF GOD

$\mathcal{S}$ eeking the Kingdom of God involves prioritizing our relationship with God. God's Kingdom must be established in *us* before we can talk about it being established anywhere else. The Kingdom of God must first reign in our body, soul, and spirit before it can reign beyond it. When the Kingdom of God reigns in our body, it will determine and affect what we do. When the Kingdom of God reigns in our soul, it will affect what we feel. Our emotions come under the authority of Jesus Christ. Uncontrolled emotions— which typically lead to sin—subject to the Kingdom of God. When the Kingdom of God reigns in our soul, it will affect our thinking. The word indicates that we must have the mind of

Christ; and that our thinking must conform to the word of God. When the Kingdom of God reigns in our soul, it will affect our will. This will result in absolute surrender and obedience to the will of God. Finally, when the Kingdom of God reigns in our spirit, it yields to God and worships Him freely.

The Kingdom of God must bring about the *character* of God. God has called us to holiness, righteousness, and integrity, so it is at times embarrassing to see the state of sin that exists in the Church. We are not perfect, and thank God for grace and mercy, but we need to understand that we are saved to be conformed to the image of Jesus Christ. Through the Holy Spirit; God has given us the capacity to overcome sin and live a victorious Christian life, so accessing the Kingdom of God must result in being filled with and controlled by the Holy Spirit. Kingdom life is spiritual life, a life that is saturated and dominated by the Holy Spirit.

In prioritizing our relationship with God, we must refocus on and emphasize spiritual disciplines. The Bible indicates that the early Church was committed to the apostles' teachings, fellowship, the breaking of bread, and prayer.

These are the rudiments of Kingdom living. The Apostles' teachings show us that we must invest in studying, knowing, and living out the word of God. Fellowship speaks to the gathering of the saints, which is critical to our edification and the edification of others. The breaking of bread most likely refers to the Lord's Supper, a supremely spiritual act that testifies to the grace and sacrifice of our Lord. Prayer is the means by which we connect to God to release His purpose in the earth.

Prioritize the Kingdom over everyone and everything else — we need to see the world through Kingdom eyes rather than through a traditionally religious perspective. For one thing, the church is not synonymous with the Kingdom. When we equate the church with the Kingdom, we blinker ourselves, and tend to prioritize our local church and denomination over the universal Church of Christians. We become overly concerned with personal church matters rather than bringing transformation to the community and wanting to see God's Kingdom established.

What do you love? Jesus said if you love anyone or anything more than Him then you are not worthy of Him. The Kingdom of God is meant to saturate all areas of our lives, and all life must be governed by divine principles and influences. Today, Christians are consumed with various things; be it worries about career advancement, financial concerns, or sources of entertainment. These things can factor into the kingdom of God if we yield all of our lives to God, but what we ought to be consumed with is the glory of God.

We are created to bring God glory, and as some would add, to bring God pleasure. What we ought to be consumed with is our purpose in God. Many Christians would struggle to articulate what these purposes are, because we become so self-absorbed that we don't see them. Our focus ought to be on God's mission. Jesus declared His mission is to seek and save those who are lost, and to teach and preach the Kingdom of God. That mission has not changed. We cannot truly talk about the Kingdom of God and minimize the importance of world evangelization, because God's first act of reconciliation is toward man, and He has to reach them somehow!

Putting God first allows all areas of our life to come into correct alignment so that divine order is established. In life, there is always something that has to come first, and that should always be God.

We often hear preachers say God must come first, then our spouse, our children and so on. We say it, but do we believe it, and more importantly do we *practice* it? When we prioritize the Kingdom of God, God moves on our behalf so that all areas of our life fall into their respective places. Unfortunately, there are too many Christians whose lives continue not to be in order because they have the wrong priorities. Matthew 6:33 states "But seek ye first the kingdom of God and His righteousness and all these things shall be added unto you", telling us that the King and His Kingdom must take first place in our lives at all times.

This applies to churches as much as it does our lives and faith. When we don't have the right priorities, the church becomes dysfunctional; resulting in stagnation and decline.

The right priorities always bring the right results. Many of us are familiar with the Pareto principle, which states that 20% of your efforts bring 80% of your results. It is therefore our responsibility to identify those things that bring us the results that we need. This principle can be applied to the activities in all major areas of our lives to help us in the process of finding God's Kingdom. Let's look at eight statements that encapsulate some key aspects of the Kingdom.

1. Kingdom Is The Sovereign Rule Of God

When Jesus introduced the Kingdom to His disciples, He spoke about the rule of God that exists in heaven, and that this rule is now to be expressed on Earth.

"Our father who is in heaven, hallowed be your name. Your kingdom comes, your will be done on earth as it is in heaven" (Matthew 6:9-13). In other words, being a Christian and disciple of Christ is about heaven invading Earth through our lives, not about us escaping Earth to go to heaven. As it has been put previously, all the major events that followed Jesus' inauguration of the kingdom—the resurrection and ascension of Jesus and the gift of the Spirit— enables us to become agents of change in the earth.

What are the implications of God's sovereignty for us? After His resurrection, Jesus said, "All authority in heaven and earth has been given to me" (Matthew 28:18), and this means that every part of creation is subject to Christ.

Abraham Kuyper put it well when he said "There is not one square inch of the entire creation about which Jesus Christ does not cry out, 'This is mine! This belongs to me!'" This means all life is sacred, and to divide the world into sacred and secular domains is to deny the sovereignty of God.

God rules over all of His creation, and there are many spheres within it. Each of these spheres can be influenced by the redemptive, compassionate, and loving servanthood of people of the Kingdom. Furthermore, all life relates to God, and what happens in each sphere of life is equally important. To serve in the marketplace of these spheres is a calling just like it is to be in church ministry.

2. Kingdom Is A Present Reality

When Jesus began his ministry he said: "The kingdom of God is at hand". Later on, He discussed things that were to happen in the future of the kingdom.

What we see here is an important principle of the Kingdom. It is both 'now' and 'not yet'. There is a tension here that needs to be recognized. If we focus solely on the 'now' of the Kingdom, we reduce it to social action alone, and if we focus purely on the 'not yet' aspect, we fail to address the current needs of the world, when in reality, it goes far beyond both of those.

Jesus saw that the ministry of the Kingdom was fulfilling the prophecy in Isaiah 61, and in Luke 4:18-19 Jesus outlines the integral and holistic nature of the Kingdom. What He professes is good news for those who may be disinherited physically, socially, politically or spiritually, as it demonstrates that the Kingdom relates to every level of human life.

The Hebrew word 'shalom' aptly describes the result of the Kingdom coming to a person or a community. It means "the establishment of peace between man and God and the well-being, welfare, or safety of an individual or a community."

Our challenge as Christians is to know what the will of God is, and to work with God by the power of the Holy Spirit to see it happen on earth.

Commenting on Matthew 6:10; NT Wright—one of the leading theologians of our time—observes that

"It's a prayer about God's kingdom coming on earth—which, as we have seen, pretty much sums up what Christianity is all about."

Simply put, Christianity can be summarized as seeing God's kingdom come on earth.

3. The Church Is Not the Kingdom

An important question must then be asked—if the Kingdom is the central message of the gospels and summarizes the essential heart of Christianity, why do we hear so little about the Kingdom of God from the pulpit or in the books we read and the DVDs we watch?

The answer is quite simple—we have substituted the Church for the Kingdom. In other words, many Christians believe what God is doing in the earth is predominantly expressed through the Church, so the gospel has been reduced to the gospel of salvation, not the gospel of the Kingdom. As a result, much of Christian thinking has been focused on individual salvation and the building up of the Church.

Amongst other things, such thinking shows a lack of understanding of the nature of God's sovereignty.

God exercises His sovereignty in two ways; saving grace, and common grace. As agents of saving grace, Christians are to evangelize and bring people to Christ. "As agents of God's common grace, we are called to help sustain and renew His creation, to uphold the created institutions of family and society, to pursue science and scholarship, to create works of art and beauty, and to heal and help those suffering from the results of the Fall." (Colson)

We see this principle in the commissions given to us by Jesus. In what is called the "Great Commission" there is the call to evangelism and discipleship, while in the "Great Commandment" we are called to love our neighbor which includes social action.

4. The Kingdom Is Within Every Person

When Jesus spoke to the Pharisees in Luke 17:21, He made another important observation about the Kingdom; He said to them "the kingdom is in your midst" - referring to Himself, but this can also be translated to mean "the kingdom of God is within you."

This concept is reiterated by Paul in Romans when he says "that which is known about God is evident within them" (Romans 1:17). Likewise, Kant wrote "Two things strike me with awe, the starry heavens above and the moral law within."

We are made to obey the laws of the Kingdom. Like the law of gravity, these laws operate whether we acknowledge them or not. For example, why does it feel good when we do good? Dr. Adler, a Jewish psychiatrist, states "I suppose all the ills of human personality can be traced back to one thing—not understanding the meaning of the phrase 'It is more blessed to give than to receive'."

This phrase sums up how the Kingdom operates. Similarly, when we make choices that hurt others, we experience inner disquiet because we are working against the truth of God that is within us. Living against the laws of the Kingdom affects our health.

Psychiatrist William Sadler put it this way; "If we lived in a truly Christian way, half the diseases of the people of America would drop off tomorrow morning and we would stand up a new healthy people."

Because we are made in the image of God, each of us has within us what Wright calls 'the echoes of the Spirit'. He identifies these as four characteristics:

- Longing for justice
- Quest for spirituality
- Hunger for relationships
- Delight in beauty

5. Kingdom Happens Outside the Church

Most Kingdom activity will take place outside Church. In fact, let's go even further—the activity of the Holy Spirit is not restricted to those places where Christians are active, because the Holy Spirit can and does speak and work within the lives of those who have not yet met the King of the Kingdom.

Take some clear examples from the book of Acts. Phillip is in the midst of a revival when the Holy Spirit directs him to go into the dessert. There, Phillip meets a leader from Ethiopia who just happens to be reading Isaiah 53 and is wondering who the prophecy is talking about. Clearly, the Holy Spirit was at work there long before Phillip came onto the scene. What made it a significant moment from a Kingdom perspective was Phillip's obedience and willingness to be in the right place at the right time to work with the Holy Spirit.

A similar theme emerges in the story of Cornelius; a God-fearing Roman centurion who is visited by an angel and directed to send men to Jerusalem to get Peter to come to his house. Peter struggles with this situation, because the work of the Kingdom initiated by the Holy Spirit is happening in a realm outside his frame of reference.

It is an important principle of the Kingdom to be able to recognize and work with the activity of the Holy Spirit as He moves into new spheres.

If we reduce the Kingdom by limiting the scope within which the Holy Spirit can work, then we limit the effectiveness of the gospel. Rather, we should be asking God to show us where the Holy Spirit is already at work within our communities, and then be looking for ways to work with Him for the expansion of the Kingdom.

When it comes to the Church, we can think of Sunday as the Church 'gathered' and Monday as the Church 'scattered'. When we do, Sunday then becomes a time to strengthen, encourage, and equip Christians to take the Kingdom into their world.

As church growth expert Eddie Gibbs says, churches should shift from a 'come' style invitational strategy to a 'go' strategy of member dispersal, with a sustained commitment to infiltrating each segment of the fragmenting world.

6. Kingdom is Expressed in a Variety of Passions

As we have established, the kingdom is all about the will of God being done on Earth. For this to happen, "God's passion must become our passion" (Wright). When we consider the nature and character of God we recognize that His passions are broad and diverse, so the Kingdom will also be expressed in a wide variety of passions.

Each member of the Godhead has taken the lead during the creation of God's Kingdom. The Father took the lead in Creation, the Son in salvation, and the Holy Spirit in completing the work that was begun through the Incarnation. Therefore, we can link the three great commissions to each member of the Trinity.

It follows from this that each of the mandates of Christianity reflect different aspects of the Kingdom. The Creation mandate puts a strong emphasis on social justice, dominion, arts, and politics; while the evangelistic mandate focuses on evangelism and discipleship. Finally, the relational mandate focuses on spiritual power, signs, and wonders.

Here we have explained three different streams within the Christian tradition—the liberals, Evangelicals, and the Pentecostals. Each stream validly represents different Godly passions.

Once we see the vastness of the Kingdom, we are given a renewed understanding of how other people can be equally as passionate as we are about what matters to us about a range of issues that may not stir our hearts, along with the fact that this passion is an expression of the heart of God for His creation. We are to pursue the passion God has given us, and equally validate and appreciate the passion He has put in others.

7. Kingdom Fruit is More Than Evangelism

Mark is a psychologist who specializes in neurofeedback therapy for Autism Spectrum conditions. Neurofeedback is a non-invasive, painless, and fun therapy for children on the Spectrum that is based on complex scientific processes. Mark's dedication to this field of study was initiated by the journey he and Kym have walked with their son Nathan.

He has seen amazing results in families that have otherwise been torn apart by trying to cope with children suffering from these conditions, yet despite these great results, Mark made this comment: "The little voice says 'what's the point of all this if they don't actually get saved and become Christians?'..."

This brings us to the question, what *is* Kingdom's fruit? Is what Mark does the produce of the Kingdom, or does it only become borne of God's Kingdom if someone makes a personal commitment to Jesus?

Many Christians would claim the latter, as they believe that only personal salvation matters to God. But is this what scripture teaches? When asked to explain how we should fulfill the great commandment to love our neighbor, Jesus used the illustration of the Good Samaritan. Nowhere in that story is there the suggestion that seeing the wounded man saved is the measure by which fulfilment of the commandment will be measured. The ministry of Jesus is summarized in Acts, where we are told that He went about doing good and healing those who were oppressed (Acts 10:38).

While it's always possible to swing towards social action and to neglect an emphasis on evangelism, I believe it is wrong to say that those who promote justice, healing, compassion, and mercy from a Christian perspective are not reflecting the heart of God and thus producing the fruit of the Kingdom. As they do this, they are sowing seeds of hope and salvation that will in many cases turn people's hearts towards encountering for themselves the reality of a personal relationship with the King of the Kingdom.

8. Every Christ Follower is an Agent for the Kingdom

For many Christians, the highlight of their week is the Sunday service, but sadly, many also believe this is where the Kingdom of God is primarily expressed, and ministry is confined to that which is done within the church. This is demonstrated in the true story of a young lawyer who was asked what her ministry was. She replied "I teach Sunday school at my church" What a travesty! In her mind, nothing she did during the week to bring justice, compassion, and resolution to the world in which she worked had spiritual value.

How can we change people's thinking to break free of this Sunday/Monday dichotomy?

Our faith makes us responsible for bringing the Kingdom into every area of life. In the words of Justine, a Burundian living in Rwanda, "I see what Jesus meant by the kingdom of God. I see that it's about changing this world, not just escaping it and retreating into our churches. If Jesus' message of the kingdom of God is true, then everything must change. Everything must change."

What a profound insight! When the Kingdom is expressed, *everything* must change. The change begins in us, and then it finds its expression in the world in which we live and work. It is about bringing God's mercy, compassion, justice, and righteousness into every sphere of His creation, so our lawyer friend has the opportunity and

33

responsibility to bring about change in her field by using her gifts, training, and experience to be an agent for change—an agent for the Kingdom.

To illustrate how this happens, Jesus used the parable of the wheat and tares (Matthew 13:36-43). In the terms of this parable, the field is the world, and He sows people of the Kingdom into the field to produce the Kingdom itself, and it is in this context that the will of God is done on Earth.

Chapter 3

THE KEY INGREDIENT TO SUCCESSFULLY MANIFEST THE KINGDOM

Faith in God is something everyone needs if they want to please the Creator. The Bible says that "Without faith, it is impossible to please God" (Hebrews 11:6). According to this view, no amount of good works you can ever do will impress the God of the Bible. You can give to worthy charities, you can be carbon-neutral in all you do, and you can live a reasonably moral life, but as long as you doubt the things He is trying to tell you, and you insist on going your own way and doing your own thing, you cannot please Him. The only way to please God according to the Bible is to believe in, accept, and follow the messenger,

He sent Jesus Christ, the Son of God, so once you put your faith in Jesus, you can start to enjoy everything God wanted you to have.

According to Christian teaching, the fundamental problem of humanity is our estrangement from Almighty God. The Bible teaches that the heart of man is naturally wicked and rejects what God is saying, and that God has made the Universe in such a way that you have to seek Him if you are going to find Him. He has made it so that those who prefer not to see Him can avoid knowing Him in many cases, and He has not even made it impossible to doubt His existence for those who prefer to think that way. However, what you or I think does not change the ultimate reality of what is actually there, and for those who have taken God at His word and sought Him out, or responded to His calling, amazing results have followed.

The problem with being estranged from God and hostile towards Him and all He says is that ultimately, divine judgment will come.

The Bible says that the wages of sin is death are that all liars, idolaters, sexually immoral people, practitioners of the occult, and so on, will end up punished in the Lake of Fire (c.f Revelation 21:8). This is obviously not a good way to end up.

The first benefit of faith, then, is that through faith you can receive forgiveness for your sins, and you can be accepted back into God's family. The Bible explicitly teaches this in Ephesians 2:8-9, which says: "For by grace you have been saved through faith, and that not of yourselves; it is the gift of God, not of works, lest anyone should boast."

Faith will get you out of trouble with God, because God has done something for us first. What God actually did was take our punishment and curse for us in our place, which was essentially what happened when Jesus died on the cross.

"For Christ also suffered once for sins, the just for the unjust, that He might bring us to God" (1 Peter 3:18) When you truly put your faith in Jesus Christ, you get the benefit of forgiveness from God, and even adoption into God's family. This is truly amazing when you think about it. There are other benefits of faith, too. Faith brings answered prayer; it can bring physical healing, and it destroys the power of fear and satan. Faith also moves the heart of God to provide for our needs in often supernatural ways.

Putting the ingredient of faith in place will yield citizenship of the Kingdom from a believer because it will cause a Kingdom lifestyle to activate both in and through them.

Making Faith a Full-Time Occupation

Hebrews 11:1 tells us that faith is the substance (the actual matter of a thing which is **REAL**, something we can see, feel and touch) of things hoped for, and the evidence of things not seen. In other words, by faith, what we pray and hope for according to the divine will, heart, and plan of God *will* happen.

When we submit to the Lordship of Christ and become *one* with him, our desires change to his, and after that point, when we have faith, hope, or pray for something, it's not empty or wishful thinking. The substance of it already exists in spirit, which is eternal, not temporal like things that occur naturally. Our job is to continue to declare and profess our faith until we see it show up and manifest in the natural world. We are his hands and feet on the Earth, here to materialize His will.

His plans and purpose are birthed through our earthen vessels, even though we can't see it in the natural world. As long as we hold fast to what he has revealed to us and what we believe to be real and true, at the appointed time, it shall come to pass for all to see.

Now let's deal with the word **full-time**, which of course means "requiring all or a large part of our time." To simplify things, let's use this example. When we fill out a job application, it often asks if we are able to work full-time or part-time. The purpose of this question is to find out our *level of commitment* to that particular position. In this situation, our response will determine the level of benefits we will receive.

It works the same in the Kingdom to a certain degree. The only difference is that our King does not accept part-time citizens or followers. Part-time means we're on the fence and have not made up our mind on whether we want to serve Him or the enemy. That's called being lukewarm. Revelation 3:15-16 says "I know your deeds, that you are neither cold nor hot. I wish you were either one or the other! So, because you are lukewarm--neither hot nor cold--I am about to spit you out of My mouth". From this, it becomes clear that He has a preference for those who are full-time, always on fire for Him, always willing and promptly obedient. If we fulfill this criteria, then we will eat the good of the land, as Isaiah 1:19 states.

There is *no* such thing as being part-time in the Kingdom! Part-time simply means we don't fully trust the Master to be our all or completely believe the promises in His word. If we are part-time, whenever we read the word and pray, we do not have the capacity to hold what we've spoken or read because we have a divided heart, or are double-minded. James 1:6-8 says it this way: "But let him ask in faith, nothing wavering (unsteady, unreliable, undecided). For he that wavereth is like a wave of the sea driven with the wind and tossed (anything and anyone sounds good and appeals to them). For let NOT that man think (not even a small consideration) that he shall receive any thing of the Lord."

This passage shows that a "double-minded" individual with divided allegiances is unstable in all his ways. For the King, being full-time entails surrendering all of ourselves and all of our time, not just a portion! We are always on-call, like a doctor who has to be prepared when their pager goes off at any time, no matter where they are. They *must* go to work when duty calls, and they signed up for the job with this understanding.

It's the same thing when we become a citizen of the Kingdom of God. We sign up to be available to the King however and whenever He chooses. Our answer should always be "YES! Holy Ghost, what would you like us to do today?" There are NO benefits for part-timers in the Kingdom of God!

Ponder this for a moment: If God decided to be part-time with us, how would that affect our lives?

What More Does The Bible Say About Faith?

Arguably, no other component of a believer's life is as important as faith. We cannot purchase it, sell it, or give it to our friends. But what is faith, and what role does faith play in the Kingdom? The dictionary defines faith as "belief in, devotion to, or trust in somebody or something, especially without logical proof." It also defines faith as "belief in and devotion to God." According to the Bible, faith is belief in the one true God without ever actually seeing Him.

There are many different measures and degrees of faith, all given to us by God, and each with a different grace and purpose. The Bible says that "EVERY man is given a measure of faith" (Romans 12:3). As believers—or Christ followers—we're all given "saving faith" purely for salvation (Ephesians 2:8-9), but there is also the spiritual GIFT of faith, which has not been given to all (I Corinthians 12:9). This spiritual gift of faith was given to edify those who are part of the body of Christ (I Corinthians 12:7). One with this gift has a relentless and unshakeable ability to believe the promises of God, and will use risky and unconventional ways to demonstrate their faith. They put the Kingdom on display at all costs!

This gift can be seen in the life of those patriarchs in Hebrews 11, but has been paramount in our own lives throughout this journey. It causes us to "walk by faith and not by our sight" regardless of the circumstances we find ourselves in, and every time we do, we've watched our faith produce the seemingly impossible! "Our faith is our currency in the kingdom." (Schmaltz, 2014) We should never be satisfied with staying at one level, and as we grow in our relationship and experience with Jesus our King, we should move from "faith to faith" (Romans 1:17). In the Kingdom of God, our King is glorified when we progress and prosper on all levels.

God designed a way to distinguish between those who belong to Him and those who don't, and that is faith. We need faith to please God, because God tells us that it pleases Him that we believe in Him even though we cannot see Him.

A key part of Hebrews 11:6 tells us that "He rewards those who earnestly seek Him." This is not to say that we choose to have faith in God just to get something from Him, but rather that God loves to bless those who are obedient and faithful. We see a perfect example of this in Luke 7:50; Jesus is engaged in dialogue with a sinful woman when He gives us a glimpse of why faith is so rewarding, and says "Your faith has saved you; go in peace." The woman believed in Jesus Christ through faith, and He rewarded her for it.

Furthermore faith is what sustains us to the end, as we know that through faith we will be in heaven with Christ our King for all eternity: "Though you have not seen Him, you love Him; and even though you do not see Him now, you believe in Him and are filled with an inexpressible and glorious joy, for you are receiving the goal of your faith, the salvation of your souls" (1 Peter 1:8-9).

Hebrews chapter 11 is known as the "faith chapter", because in it, great deeds of faith are described. By faith, Abel offered a pleasing sacrifice to the Lord (v. 4); by faith, Noah prepared the ark in a time when rain was unknown (v. 7); by faith, Abraham left his home and obeyed God's command to go where he knew not, then willingly offered up his only son (vv. 8-10, 17); by faith, Moses led the children of Israel out of Egypt (vv. 23-29); by faith, Rahab received the spies of Israel and saved her life (v. 31).

Many more heroes "who through faith conquered kingdoms, administered justice, and gained what was promised; who shut the mouths of lions, quenched the fury of the flames, and escaped the edge of the sword; whose weakness was turned to strength; and who became powerful in battle and routed foreign armies" (vv. 33-34) are aliso mentioned in this chapter. Clearly, the existence of faith is demonstrated by **action**!

According to the Bible, faith is essential to lead a successful life in the Kingdom. Without a demonstration of our faith and trust in God, we have no place with Him, because we only believe in God's existence by faith.

Most people have a vague, disjointed notion of who God is, so they lack reverence for His exalted position in their lives. These people lack the true faith needed to have an eternal relationship with God the Father through Christ, who loves them and gave His life for them. Our faith will suffer times of trial and testing in order to prove that it is authentic, as well as to sharpen and strengthen it. This is why James tells us to "consider it pure joy when we fall into trials, because the testing of our faith produces perseverance and matures us, providing the evidence that our faith is real" (James 1:2-4).

In Matthew 17:20 Jesus said, "Because you have so little faith. I tell you the truth, if you have faith as small as a mustard seed, you can say to this mountain, 'Move from here to there' and it will move. **NOTHING WILL BE IMPOSSIBLE FOR YOU.**"

Let's attempt to do this faith exercise. Try to convince yourself that God exists. It doesn't work, because that is like trying to convince your shadow that the sun exists. In believing what you do not see; the reward of faith is the opportunity to see what you believe, but true faith is known within your heart, beyond the reach of proof.

Chapter 4

WAYS TO MANIFEST THE KINGDOM

$\mathcal{T}$his will be done with scripture and making some analogies to explicate Matthew 6:33, which states, "But seek first his kingdom and his righteousness, and all these things will be added to you".

We see many zealous believers who are actively involved in God's work at first, but eventually lose their enthusiasm, interest, and desire to pay the price of that involvement, and subsequently fall away. In these cases, they lose not only their first love and the fire of the Holy Spirit, but God altogether. Zeal alone is not enough to demonstrate the Kingdom of God effectively. To do so, you first need to work on yourself so that the features of the

King—i.e. His views, attitudes and behavior—and the values of the Kingdom reign in you. Of course, it is important to do good things, to be compassionate, to care for the needy, but working on ourselves to imitate the image of God is of primary importance.

Matthew 6:33 says that most of our attention and efforts should be directed towards seeking the Kingdom of God, and all that we need will become available to us, so what does it mean to seek the Kingdom of God? Where can we find it?

The word "kingdom" has two meanings: 1) the reign of a king and 2) the territory where he reigns. The King of the Kingdom of God is Jesus, so we must seek Him and crave Him. "As the deer pants for the water brooks, so my soul pants for You, O God", exclaims the psalmist. Our soul must be filled with God, and always seeking Him, and this will help to transform us into true disciples and citizens in His Kingdom.

The sons and heirs of the kingdom need to live in constant communion with the Lord, every minute of every day. "To keep a lamp burning, we have to keep putting oil in it", as Mother Teresa used to say. Luke 17:21 tells us that "the kingdom of God is within us", so if we cannot find God deep inside our heart, it is unlikely that we will find Him outside it. We probably would not recognize Him even if we were to meet Him face to face, hence, we cannot manifest Him on Earth. That is why Jesus wants us to become like Him, filled with Him, and imitate Him.

Due to Genesis 1:27, we know that God created us in His image and likeness, which should be revealed in our character, beliefs, behaviors and attitudes toward people. If God is love, people need to see that we are like Him. Let them see the love in your eyes, your sincere smile, and in your paying attention to them and desire to help. If God is a spirit, we must be spiritual people. Do not judge anyone according to their flesh, but try to see God's spark in them. Do not live by earthly goals and challenges, but be focused on eternity. Let us learn from Jesus Christ in order to carry His image and reflect His nature.

Jesus had fullness of faith, humility, patience, all-conquering love, strength, sacrifice, courage, and bravery, and was perfect in holiness, so He became our King. Now it is our responsibility to carry His image, and to be effective for God here on earth, just as he was. John 12:25 states that "Anyone who loves their life will lose it, while anyone who hates their life in this world will keep it for eternal life". This verse confirms that we must work on changing our worldview to imitate the image of the Heavenly Father and to become the bearer of His nature.

John 15: 1-4 reads, "I am the true vine, and My Father is the vinedresser...Abide in me, and I in you. As the branch cannot bear fruit by itself, unless it abides in the vine, neither can you, unless you abide in Me".

We need to be grafted into the true vine—Jesus Christ himself. Only then will we be able to bring the spiritual fruits that cannot be earned by any external effort, but come forth from God's presence in us. We must pay the utmost attention to this mission and work on it with the help of prayer, the Holy Spirit, meditating on the word of God, and fellowship with other like-minded Kingdom citizens. As a tree cannot grow without soil, so we cannot live without God. As a fish cannot live without water, so we cannot live without Him.

God is the source of our holiness, faith, strength, joy, health, relief, and prosperity, and we cannot live a fulfilled and beautiful life without building a relationship with Christ. Without Him, we are doomed to a vain, sad, and unfruitful existence.

Galatians 5:22-23 says, "But the fruit of the Spirit is love, joy, peace, forbearance, kindness, goodness, faithfulness, gentleness and self-control. Against such things, there is no law." The fruit of the Spirit is the result of our communion with Christ. Let us strive to let the the Holy Spirit work in and thorugh us, to have His words on our lips, so that our words will touch the hearts of all listeners, regardless of age, social status, or religion.

The acts of the flesh which prevent our entrance to the Kingdom are obvious: "sexual immorality, impurity and debauchery; idolatry and witchcraft; hatred, discord, jealousy, fits of rage, selfish ambition, dissensions, factions and envy; drunkenness, orgies, and the like. I warn you, as I did before, that those who live like this will not inherit the kingdom of God" (Galatians 5:19-21). The Bible tells us that these acts of the flesh that originally lived in us can and should be put to death by the Spirit—"but if ye through the Spirit do mortify the deeds of the body, ye shall live" (Romans 8:13).

Our main mission is to reveal the character of Jesus—"the Son is the image of the invisible God, the firstborn over all creation" (Colossians 1:15)—in all our affairs, so that people do not grope for God, but can see Him in us and experience Him through us. We must let our surroundings learn about the true God from a fruitful life led by His followers. Our knowledge of the Bible does not convince people that God is alive but demonstrates a simple, Christ-centered Kingdom lifestyle worthy of imitation. We must represent the character of the King at home, outdoors, at school, at work and in problematic situations. We need to be filled with the need to love and seek God so that He shows up in and through us every day. Make the decision right now!

John 1:14: "The Word became flesh and made His dwelling among us. We have seen His glory, the glory of the one and only Son, who came from the Father, full of grace and truth."

God becomes our nature only when we take the

time to work on ourselves, and work relentlessly for the word to become flesh. We must strive for it with all our might. No matter how many sermons we have listened to, how many times we have read the Bible, or and how many conferences and Bible schools we have attended, the word is dead and useless to us until we start to work with God allow him to change our human nature. Through the pages of the word of God, we should see the soul of God, reflect it, and instill it in the world.

Hebrews 10: 5-7—"Therefore, when Christ came into the world, He said: 'Sacrifice and offering you did not desire, but a body you prepared for me; with burnt offerings and sin offerings you were not pleased.' Then I said, 'Here I am—it is written about me in the scroll—I have come to do your will, my God". God wants to see us capable of revealing Him, bearing His image and likeness, and reflecting His essence more than sacrifices and offerings.

May God help us to become people who can say with Jesus: "Here I am, I have come to do your will, my God". Let everyone who meets us on our way receive salvation, blessing, wisdom, understanding, and goodness.

WRITE DOWN YOUR VISION

You may well agree with us that putting down an idea is better than keeping it in your heart, not just because the heart has many other issues in it, but also because jotting your thoughts on a notepad will serve as reminder.

One must be able to write their vision down and make it plain in order to know their direction and have a blueprint to successfully build what the King has ordained for their lives. To buttress this, we turn to Habakkuk 2:2, which states "And the LORD answered me, and said, Write the vision, and make it plain upon tables, that he may run that readeth it."

This depicts that the King agrees on penning things down just to make it clearer and stand as a reminder of what the visionary and writer endeavors to accomplish. "Where there is no vision, the people perish, but happy is he who keeps the law"—Proverbs 29:18. Vision is the bridge between the present and the future, and without it, we perish or go "unrestrained," as the New American Standard Bible puts it.

Vision gives pain a purpose, and those without

vision spend their lives taking the path of least resistance as they try to avoid discomfort. The level of sacrifice that a vision requires will determine the magnitude of people who follow, and sacrifice separates the small from the great. Consider a young man who has just graduated from high school and joins the military—as soon as he steps off the bus to boot camp, the sergeant starts yelling at him, saying he has to march over to the barbershop and get his head shaved. He gets up early in the morning just to exercise with someone screaming at him and insulting his mother. Just a month before, he was in high school.

He would never have tolerated this treatment from his teachers or classmates, but somehow his whole mindset has changed. Why? He is enduring the "cross", so to speak, because of the joy and reward on the other side of it. He realizes that boot camp is preparing him for a greater destiny; his vision of the future gives his present physical discomfort meaning and purpose. Many of us go through life not understanding the purpose of our trials. We spend our days walking a crooked path, believing that every obstacle in the road is a problem and something to be avoided.

The second part of this Proverb says, "But happy is he who keeps the Law." The law isn't just something God gave to Moses, it is also the restraint, boundaries, and disciplines we develop in our lives to direct us through obstacles instead of around them. These obstacles become baptisms of fire that forge our character so we can attain and maintain a life of greatness.

What Is Vision?

Vision is not just what we see, but also *the way in which* we see. Vision is the lens that we use to interpret the events of our life, the way we view people, and our concept of God. If we have a scratch on our glasses, it may seem like everybody around us has scratches marring their vision too, but the problem actually lies with us. Jesus said that our eyes are the windows to our heart, and Paul prayed that the eyes of our understanding would be enlightened. In other words, we *perceive* with our eyes, but we *see* and interpret with our spirits.

If our heart becomes bitter, jealous, hurt, or otherwise infected, the lens of our spirit is distorted. What we perceive is happening and what is really going on could be two completely different things. Jesus said, "You will know the truth and the truth will make you free" (John 8:32). The word truth does not refer to the Bible in this context, (although all truth is rooted in the word of God) but rather *reality*. Jesus is telling us that we will understand what is real, and that will free us.

So many of us live in a virtual reality. The way we view life can feel and look real, or make perfect sense, but still not be real at all. Have you ever watched a good movie and gotten totally into it, maybe even experienced real emotions as a result of it? You may leave the theater still "feeling" the movie, but you know it was just a movie, and it was never real. The truth is that we see what we believe to be true according to our emotions, limited information, and experiences, or lack of them, and that's flawed. If you have the wrong pretext, you will misunderstand the context. Having a revelation of what is real (authentic) will deliver us from the life of torment that virtual reality often causes.

ESTABLISHING CORE VALUES

The things we believe to be true determine the ways in which we interpret life, and these beliefs are called "core values". Our core values make up the lens of our heart, through which we are constantly seeing things and making judgements. With that in mind, it is important for us to realize the incongruence between what our core values are presently and what we really want them to be. Often, the things we say we believe and the things we actually believe are not the same. We must understand that it is not the truths that we believe in our head that are our core values, but rather, the ones we believe in our heart.

These core values determine the way we respond to both the world around us and the Holy Spirit who lives within us, and helps define the part of the flock that we find ourselves called to. The children of Israel experienced this principle when they came into the Promised Land.

Joshua assigned them land according to their tribes, divisions, (Joshua 18:10) and diverse visions. For instance, if they had a vision for farming, they probably did not go with Caleb to the mountain country, and instead were given land that best facilitated their vision.

From this perspective, it isn't hard to see how some church splits happen. Sometimes, pastors, in their zeal to build their churches, attract people that have a vision for things that their churches—or "land", metaphorically speaking—will not sustain. This duality of vision eventually ends up in division.

FORESIGHT, INSIGHT & OVERSIGHT

True Godly vision consists of foresight, insight and oversight that come from His sight. Foresight is like looking at life through a telescope, and allows us to know what is ahead as it connects us to our future. It helps life make sense, and gives us the motivation that we described earlier.

Insight is like viewing life through a microscope, and gives us an understanding of why things happen, as well as helping us determine the underlying motivations of the heart.

Oversight puts life into context, and is like flying over our house in a helicopter. It offers a unique perspective that helps us understand where we are in relation to everything else. The sons of Issachar are great examples of this kind of vision.

1 Chronicles says that these men understood the times, and had knowledge of what Israel should do (12:32). People that are blessed with this type of vision often have great wisdom concerning the seasons of life. His sight assures us that the vision we have is from God, and vision from the Lord creates a mission from heaven.

This is illustrated in the life of Moses when he went up to the mountain, received a vision of the tabernacle, and was told to construct it according to the pattern that he had received. (Exodus 24:16-18) He received a vision from God, and as soon as he did, there had to be a plan of action to accomplish it. Otherwise, the dream or vision would have eventually turned into a nightmare and caused Moses' heart to grow sick.

A lot of people have lofty ideas about things they would like to accomplish for God, but they seem to have no sense of how to see the dream fulfilled. There are entire books dedicated to this subject!

Here is a brief overview of how to accomplish a vision through **PRACTICAL IMPLEMENTATION**.

The first part of accomplishing any vision is to take

it from the unseen world and bring it into this natural world. This can be accomplished by simply writing down the vision, because articulating it on paper pulls the dream that is in your spirit into the visible world so that others can capture it in their hearts. Tools that help to visualize the mission— such as architectural drawings, models, testimonies of others who have accomplished a similar vision or visits to places that have a common purpose— are all helpful in capturing and defining the vision for yourself and others who will come along to help.

Again, it's needed to reiterate here the importance of writing the vision down. "Then the LORD answered me and said, 'Record the vision and inscribe it on tablets, that the one who reads it may run. For the vision is yet for the appointed time; it hastens toward the goal and it will not fail. Though it tarries, wait for it; for it will certainly come, it will not delay"— (Habakkuk 2:2-3).

There is an old story about three bricklayers that helps illustrate what it looks like when people receive motivation from taking ownership of a vision:

There were three bricklayers working beside each other on a wall. Someone came up to the first one and said, "What are you doing?"

"What does it looks like I am doing?" the bricklayer replied sarcastically, "I am laying bricks!"

The man asked the next guy on the wall what he was doing, and he said, "Can't you see what I am doing? I am building a wall."

Then the last man was asked what he was doing, and he exclaimed, "I am building a great cathedral for God!"

Who do you think will do the best quality work and be the hardest worker? Vision causes people to love their work, because with it, they can see the big picture. Someone once said, "If you want to build a great ship, you can go out and find some talented craftsman, or you can find a person who loves the sea." Imparting God's vision to the those around us who are capable of helping us fulfill it is one of the most important factors of seeing the mission accomplished.

The next step is to create a plan to accomplish the mission.

The Bible says: "Without consultation, plans are frustrated, but with many counselors, they succeed; the plans of the heart belong to man, but the answer of the tongue is from the LORD" (Proverbs 15:22 and 16:1). From these two verses, we can see that although the vision must be from God Himself, humans are to help develop the plan that brings about the fulfillment of the vision. Notice how Solomon highlights the fact that developing plans in a vacuum—without the expertise and insight of others who have different gifts and perspectives—will ultimately end in frustration.

It's important for administrative people to understand that they are there to *add* to the mission, not change it. Visionaries do not often like to work with administrators, because by nature administrators are refiners and finishers. Sometimes, administrators do not understand that they are being brought in to help visionaries determine *how* something should be accomplished, not *what* should be accomplished. If the vision is so large that it requires the help of heaven; which it often does when it really is from God, it becomes important that the visionary imparts not only the vision to those around them, but also the faith to see it accomplished. First Timothy 1:4 says that the administration of God is "by faith."

FEAR COUNTERACTS FAITH

People often disguise their fear as wisdom when they enter into a supernatural mission that can only be accomplished with the help of God. Moses had this problem when he sent the twelve spies into the promised land to determine where they should enter. Ten of the spies misunderstood their mission and somehow thought they were being asked whether or not they should take the land at all. This type of misunderstanding of the roles people are invited to play in the mission has caused the demise of so many would-be miracles, paralyzing the Church of the living God.

For years, the Church has often settled for what can be accomplished by human effort and ability, because we have allowed the opinions of faithless people to determine what we will achieve, instead of being faithful—faith-*filled*—to the vision we saw "on the mountain." Doing so is a perversion of the gospel of the Kingdom. We should never settle for anything less than what God tells us to do.

Setting Goals

After the plan is established, goals must be set. The Bible says: "I press on toward the goal for the prize of the upward call of God in Christ Jesus" (Philippians 3:14). Goals are simply the vision being broken down into smaller pieces that are measurable by time and space. In other words, they are specified parts of the mission that will be accomplished by a predetermined date.

Many people don't like to set goals because they think that if they are not able to accomplish them on time, they have failed. The truth of the matter is that "If you fail to plan you plan to fail." Great leaders know that setting goals is what gives the mission a sense of urgency, and urgency is a friend to managers because it sets the pace for those who are carrying out the mission.

If wisdom is used in goal-setting, very little management is needed to motivate the workers, because urgency manages them. However, be careful not to give your team more than they have the faith be able to to accomplish in a given time period. If it is too much, they will not even try. It is like trying to catch a bus when it is already a block ahead; you probably won't even run after it as there is so little possibility of catching up. On the other hand, if the bus has just started to pull away from the curb when you get there, you will probably move out of your comfort zone to try to catch it. That said, it is equally important to remember that setting goals too low will not create a sense of urgency at all. People will not be very motivated, and that will result in a lot more work for the managers.

The final stage of seeing the mission accomplished to establish your steps. Proverbs says, "The mind of man plans his way, but the Lord directs his steps" (16:9). Psalms says, "The steps of a good man are established by the Lord, and He delights in his way. When he falls, he will not be hurled headlong, because the Lord is the one who holds his hand." (37:23-24). Steps are your day-in, day-out walks with God, the step-by-step, moment-by-moment, hour-by-hour decisions you make, and the things you do that require your time and energy.

When your vision is birthed by God Himself, He will be delighted to direct your steps, so the most important thing to remember about your steps is that they should be found somewhere in your mission. Go back through your planner from the previous month and retrace your steps. Does it look like they are directly attached to your mission? If not, either redefine your mission, or redirect your steps. Remember, the future is at stake!

BE A CHEERFUL GIVER

A Kingdom citizen not only should be a giver, but a cheerful giver! The Bible says in 2 Corinthians 9 that "He who sows sparingly shall reap also sparingly and he which soweth bountifully shall reap also bountifully." Verse 7 continues by saying "every man according as he purposeth in his heart, so let him give; not grudgingly, or of necessity: for God loveth a cheerful giver." Giving with a divided mind or doubt within makes the gift look like the offering of Cain, which was not accepted by God. It is essential to give with an open heart; cheerfully and joyfully, because giving outside joy seems like one is being forced to do so! As the verse above suggests, the Kingdom has its own economy and system of prospering; we can't expect to harvest an orange grove if we only sowed one orange seed! We must sow many orange seeds in order to reap a large harvest. On this journey, giving is the main reason why we will or will not have bountiful continued blessings in our lives!

Luke 6:38 gives us some insight into this: "Give, and it shall be given unto you; good measure, pressed down, and shaken together, and running over, shall men give into your bosom. For with the same measure that ye mete withal it shall be measured to you again."

This is called the principle of sowing and reaping, and there are many other scriptures to bring greater understanding on the matter of how necessary it is to be a giver in the Kingdom and the benefits to Kingdom citizens. Another important foundation to prospering in God's Kingdom is to become a faithful tither. Many people think tithing is about God needing something from us, but the truth is, tithing is God's management system for testing our faithfulness to His word. He expects us to give just ten percent of all that we have and be a good manager over the other 90% percent of our income. God does not need our money—our tithes are a security deposit to keep devastation out of our lives, and a test to see if we will keep His principles *first*, regardless of worldly things and the circumstances that arise in our lives as Kingdom citizens.

A familiar scripture on tithing is found in Malachi 3:10: "Bring ye all the tithes into the storehouse, that there may be meat in mine house, and prove me now herewith, saith the LORD of hosts, if I will not open you the windows of heaven, and pour you out a blessing, that there shall not be room enough to receive it."

It's a trust and management matter above all. When one has the right heart and proper understanding of tithing, giving, and sowing, it becomes a delight, not a dreadful task.

KINGDOM MANAGEMENT

It should be clear to all kingdom citizens that we own nothing.

God our King owns everything, and all we are doing on Earth is serving as managers over His possessions. Matthew 25:21 says, "His Lord said to him, well done, good and faithful servant: you were faithful over a few things, I will make you ruler over many things."

This scripture speaks volumes to what God requires from us. In the previous section, we talked about tithing and how God allows us to do what we want with ninety percent of our income. It's unfortunate that most believers are in a tail position because of poor management, becoming the borrower instead of the lender! Here is a secret; God will never "give you what you pray for, but what you can manage" (Monroe, 2017). Most believers feel as though they are stuck at a certain place and they are correct, because "God will stop growth where there is no management" (Monroe, 2017).

God is just, so He doesn't make rich people or poor people. Some become rich and some become poor, depending on how His resources were managed in their lives. Management will demand work! That's why He says "faith without works is dead." It's no good to be able to quote every scripture and speak in tongues, but not experience the fruit of the word. Most believers would rather live off miracles than become good managers of God's resources. Being financially embarrassed is not the will of God for a Kingdom citizen's life. Genesis 2:4-5 speaks about this very thing. God knew management was so important that He did not cause it to rain on the earth until He had man to till or manage the grounds. If God HAD allowed it to rain before He created man, imagine how everything would have grown out of place and become unmanageable for any human being!

BE A PRAYERFUL CITIZEN

We must be a people of PRAYER. In the words of Prophetess Tisha Ricks: "If you can't live without air, how can you live without prayer?"

In the Kingdom, our direct line of communication with the King is prayer. Having a fruitful prayer life helps to produce a more fulfilled, abundant and powerful life! There is a place for praise, worship, preaching, and teaching the word. As Kingdom citizens, we must incorporate all of these to experience a balanced, fruitful, purposeful life.

Prayer is our **mandate**, not an option! We must also know how to pray with aim and focus so that we don't pray or ask amiss as James 4:3 tells us. Many people in the Church are doing a lot of praying, but not many get the results they desire. WHY is this? There are many factors that stand as hindrances:

i. Prayer with no obedience causes what was promised to be withheld.

ii. Not having the right heart motives or being sincere.

iii. Having fervency with no effectualness (according to dictionary.com, effectual means being capable of producing an intended effect).

iv. You must pray with the end in mind. There must be no doubt of what you're praying for.

v. *Faith* has to be the *main* ingredient in prayer. Mark 11:24 says "Therefore I tell you, whatever you ask for in prayer, believe that you have received it, and it will be yours." Once we utter prayer, it should be in our mind that what we are praying for has already been given to us. Many in the body of Christ are praying, but don't have the faith to fully believe what they are praying for, and as we have seen before, this is called being double-minded. James 1:6-8 says it best: "but when you ask, you must believe and not doubt, because the one who doubts is like a wave of the sea, blown and tossed by the wind. That person should not expect to receive anything from the Lord. Such a person is double-minded and unstable in all they do." Faith and prayer are essential!

vi. Coupling prayer with proper fasting—especially when praying for evil spirits to be loosed from one's life—is also essential (Matthew 17:21). You need both of these power mechanisms to work together to break their hold.

There are other variables that play a role in the a Kingdom citizen having a healthy and result-filled prayer life. However, for the sake of this book, the above are some of the main components that, if put into practice, will upgrade your prayer life tremendously.

HOLY SPIRIT

This is the third Godhead; the comforter, and our teacher and guide. He is a person! As a matter of fact, "He is our governor. The MOST important person on Earth." (Monroe, 2007) It should be made known that citizens of the kingdom have no real achievement without this teacher.

"Howbeit when He, the Spirit of truth, is come, and He will guide you into all truth: for He shall not speak of Himself; but whatsoever He shall hear, that shall He speak: and He will show you things to come" (John 16:13). This same Holy Spirit helps us and gives us strength and power to fulfill our ordained assignments according to the will of God (Acts 1:4).

"And, behold, I send the promise of my Father upon you: but tarry ye in the city of Jerusalem, until ye be endued with power from on high" (Luke 24:49). This is very important; here, no man had power to do any works until they had the infilling of the Holy Spirit to assist them.

The Holy Spirit lives within us, revealing the mysteries and secrets of the Kingdom. He also helps us to live out our individual assignments the way the King originally intended.

John 14:26 " But the Comforter, which is the Holy Ghost, whom the Father will send in my name, He shall teach you all things, and bring all things to your remembrance, whatsoever I have said unto you." This particular verse demonstrates that the mysteries that can arise from God's message are made clear by the Holy Spirit.

Ephesians 6:19-20 says: "And for me, that utterance may be given unto me, that I may open my mouth boldly, to make known the mystery of the gospel. For which I am an ambassador in bonds: that therein I may speak boldly, as I ought to speak." We see here that the Holy Spirit gives us the boldness to speak the mysteries of the Kingdom. Thanks to the Holy Spirit, we can speak with assurance, clarity, and precision without fear in a way that is the mark of a true Kingdom citizen.

When the Holy Spirit is active within us, He gives us the gift of a new language, one which is essential in the Kingdom. Why? Well, because every country has its own language that they use to communicate, and it's no different in the Kingdom of God.

So, what is this language? It called tongues, or glossolalia. This language needs to be activated in every person who professes Christ their as Lord and Savior, but gives us the power necessary to function at our highest level and to fulfill what we were ordained to do.

Let's use this example: Someone has no money, but is carrying an ATM card that is linked to a bank account filled with cash. Until the person activates the card, it is useless to them, and they will remain without money that is already at their disposal.

It works the same with having the Holy Spirit living inside us. Until He is activated within us, we will never enjoy the full benefits of Him being there, and the language of the Kingdom is a sign that the Holy Spirit is truly active within us. When He is active in us, He will give us the ability to act in accordance with the Father's mind, will, and purpose for us.

DISCIPLESHIP

The root word of 'discipleship' is 'disciple', but what is a disciple?

The standard definition of a disciple is someone who adheres to the teachings of another in the capacity of a follower or a learner. As it applies in the Kingdom, where Jesus is our King, a disciple is someone who learns of Him, and endeavors to live, talk, walk, and act like Him. Because of God's awakening grace, they begin to conform every part of their ways to the ways of Jesus.

In the kingdom, we must become "imitators of Christ", who are obedient and 100% sold out to Him. The four Gospels give us a definitive portrait of Jesus' life on Earth, so if we really want to know what it means to be His disciple, the Gospels are where we should start.

In particular, John's Gospel shows us three complimentary perspectives on what it means to follow Jesus, each patterned after Jesus Himself. Building off of John's profile, we could say that a disciple of Jesus is a commited follower, worshipper, and a witness.

To be clear, a disciple is not satisfied with merely following religion and showing up in a "church" building a few times a week because they understand that *we are the church*. Again, just showing up in and of itself does not produce a life that can be deemed as Kingdom, nor does it produce the abundance and fruitfulness that pleases the King.

A disciple must be wholeheartedly devoted to follow the King no matter the cost. We must be willing to forsake everything for His will. Jesus demonstrated this in Luke 22:42 when He said: "Father, if thou be willing, remove this cup from

Me: nevertheless, not My will, but thine will be done." He was willing to do His father's will no matter what!

He also went further in John 4:34: "Jesus saith unto them, My meat is to do the will of Him who sent Me, and to finish His work." He was saying here "the greatest thing that brings nourishment to My body is to do the Father's will." That must be our stance in this life, and the way we truly prove that the Kingdom of God has penetrated our hearts and been *awakened* **within us**. Nothing else should take precedence over fulfilling what our King has sent us to earth to accomplish! "We cannot return unto Him void." (Isaiah 55:11)

These are some characteristics that Kingdom disciples should possess:

i. They love Jesus above everyone and everything. The first Commandment calls for us as disciples of Christ to adhere to this with devotion. While disciples love their family, friends, and even foes, they put the Lord above all else; and that's evident in their priorities. Money, career progression, and ambition may be a part of their lives, but these material interests never come before Christ, following His commandments, or being a doer of His Word.

ii.   They are selfless and understand the importance of sacrifice.

iii. They exemplify humility and modesty just as Jesus did. He made Himself of no reputation because He knew who He was and didn't have anything to prove. They are not haughty or prideful, as they know this is what will cause them "destruction and to fall" (James 4:6). Being humble does not mean one walks around with their head hung low, walking very softly, but rather that you are under the submission of God, you know who you are and *are* who you are to the Glory of God.

iv.   A disciple understands that without the Holy Spirit they are nothing and can do nothing in and of themselves. They know they have need of Him in order to fulfill what He has given them to accomplish.

v.   They are dedicated to following Christ, His commandments and loving one another.

John 13:35 says it this way: "By this shall all men know that ye are my disciples if ye have love one to another." John 8:31-32 also says: If you continue in my word, you are truly My disciples; and you will know the truth, and the truth will make you free."

vi.   They are not easily influenced by the world or its standards. "They are in the world but not of it" (John 17:16).

vii.   They have self-control in their emotions and actions. This is evident in the way they behave, regardless of how others act toward them. If criticized, ridiculed, or persecuted for their faith, they respond with kindness, just as Jesus did, and know that it is a privilege to be persecuted for the sake of the Christ and His Kingdom (I Peter 3:13-17).

viii. A disciple lives the word. They are a light that shines in the world and reflects the Lord in their actions and lifestyle. Their faith is reflected in their words and deeds. Jesus said in Matthew 5:14-16 "You are the light of the world. A city built on a hill cannot be hidden. No one after lighting a lamp puts it under the bushel basket, but on the lampstand, and it gives light to all in the house. In the same way, let your light shine before others, so that they may see your good works and give glory to your Father in heaven."

ix.   A disciple professes the word regularly and effectively. They speak the word of the Lord in regular conversation, not in a preachy way, but naturally, because it's what they live and believe. They are eager to share the word because their desire is to introduce the Lord to everyone. "They become a living epistle read of all men." (2 Corinthians 3:1-3)

UNDERSTAND SONSHIP

We must understand that we have been given an inheritance to become *sons* of God, not just servants as some claim. When we speak of a son, it is not in reference to a male. It has to do with our spiritual inheritance as citizens in God's kingdom. There is an adoption that happens when we receive Jesus as Lord and Savior. It is called sonship. Ephesians 1:5 says "He predestined us for adoption as sons through Jesus Christ, according to the purpose of

His will. Galatians 4:7 says "Wherefore thou art no more a servant, but a son; and if a son, then an heir of God through Christ." John 15:15-16 goes further when he states "Henceforth I call you not servants; for the servant knoweth not what his Lord doeth: but I have called you friends; for all things that I have heard of my Father I have made known unto you. Ye have not chosen Me, but I have chosen you, and ordained you, that ye should go and bring forth fruit, and that your fruit should remain: that whatsoever ye shall ask of the Father in My name, He may give it you."

We are not weak, downtrodden people! We are heirs of the promise. That means we are heirs to what's His, namely "the earth and the fullness thereof". (Psalm 24:1)

Galatians 3:29: "And if ye be Christ's, then are ye Abraham's seed, and heirs according to the promise."

We have been given the dominion and authority to reign over and subdue the Earth just like the King, Christ Jesus. Genesis 1:26-28 says, "And God said, let Us make man in our image, after our likeness: and let them have dominion over the fish of the sea, and over the fowl of the air, and over the cattle, and over all the earth, and over every creeping thing that creepeth upon the earth. So God created man in His own image, in the image of God He created them; male and female He created them. And God blessed them, and God said unto them, be fruitful, and multiply, and replenish the earth, and subdue it: and have dominion over the fish of the sea, and over the fowl of the air, and over every living thing that moveth upon the earth."

Because we are made in His likeness and in His image, we have the same power that Jesus possessed to control all faculties on earth and in heaven. We are not subject to the prince of this world—the enemy—but rather he is subject to *us*, because of the *greater* one who lives within us.

The enemy is a "defeated foe", according to the word of God, and when we truly understand who we are and the power we possess, his only recourse is to attempt to buffet us because he knows he has no power to stop us!

When a citizen of the Kingdom becomes aware of who they are, they become a weapon of mass destruction to the kingdom of darkness. Through this, an individual who is a citizen of God's Kingdom can make the enemy their footstool, according to Romans 16:20: "And the God of peace shall bruise satan under your feet shortly."

All Kingdom citizens have been given the ability to bind and loose, not just what's on Earth but also that which is in heaven (Matthew 18:18). However, if we continue walking through life unconscious of this, we forfeit this authority, and become an open target for all the wicked devices of the enemy. That is not our lot as a citizen of God's Kingdom!

EPILOGUE

There is always more to learn concerning the kingdom of God, its functioning, and how it relates to our life, but our assignment with this book was to use the immense experiences, wisdom, knowledge and revelation that we've gained over decades to bring about an awakening in those who are tired of religion; and all the politics, wrong thinking, and erroneous teaching that has surrounded it for years. Religion has, for centuries, kept people bound, blind, stagnant and ignorant of the dominion and true power they possess WITHIN to fulfill their God-ordained assignments, as well as how to effectively use that power, dominion and their gifts to make a mighty impact on the world around them. We pray that through reading this book you have become so ignited with truth that you are ready to let go of religious thinking and **AWAKEN** to the Kingdom Within You!

Kingdom Blessings,

Apostle Corey & Prophetess Tisha Ricks, CPC.

Sources for Scriptures

The Holy Bible: King James Version,
Second Edition. Thomas Nelson, 2013.

King James Version. 1993. BibleGateway.com.

King James Version. 2012. BibleHub.com.

Kingdom Reformation
Ministries Worldwide

www.kingdomreformationministries.com

Made in the USA
Lexington, KY
13 November 2019